NOTION®
Conducting Workbook

3rd Edition

Prepared by

Dr. Jack Jarrett
and the Notion Music Team

About the Author

Dr. Jarrett is both a composer and conductor. As a Fulbright student in 1962-63, he studied operatic conducting under Professor Erich Peter at the Berlin Hochschule für Musik. Further conducting studies were with Tibor Kozma and Julius Herford at Indiana University (1964-65), and later as a Conducting Fellow in Aspen, Colorado (1980). He conducted both choruses and orchestra at the University of North Carolina-Greensboro (1965-74) and at Virginia Commonwealth University (1974-1980). In 1980, following a national search, he was named Assistant Conductor of the Richmond, Virginia Symphony Orchestra. In 1989 he was appointed Chair of the Composition and Conducting Department at Berklee College of Music in Boston, where for the next decade he innovated the use of computer technology for teaching orchestral conducting. In 2001, he left Berklee to launch NOTION Music, Inc., with a line of music software products he designed.

Acknowledgements

This workbook benefited from extensive collaboration and assistance from Dr. David Oertel, conductor and educator, and Mr. Lubo Astinov, film composer and educator.

Samples for playback were recorded by the London Symphony Orchestra at Abbey Road Studios in London. Abbey Road and the Abbey Road logo are trademarks of EMI Records Limited and are used under license. London Symphony Orchestra and LSO logo are trademarks of London Symphony Orchestra Ltd, registered in the UK, US, and other countries.

For more information and support, go to: www.presonus.com/products/notion-conducting

---

Notion by PreSonus

Notion for Mac and Windows

As well as Notion Conducting software, check out Notion, our full notation package. Available on Windows and Mac, it features the same live performance capability as Notion Conducting, as well as being able to create and edit scores from scratch. Easy to use, great sounding, and compatible with other notation software via MusicXML.

www.presonus.com/products/notion-5

Notion for iOS (iPad & iPhone)

Head to the App Store and search for Notion, to create and edit your music on the move. Sync with Notion desktop via iCloud, DropBox or email. Play back with the great LSO sounds you've heard in Notion Conducting. Share full score and parts as Notion files or as pdf.

www.presonus.com/products/notion-for-ios

PreSonus

Check out presonus.com for a full range of mixers, monitor speakers, audio interfaces and recording and mixing software. Add a pair of Ceres™ or Eris speakers, an iTwo Studio bundle and a Faderport to your home or school workstation - or complete your software needs with the award winning Studio One® DAW.

www.presonus.com

TABLE OF CONTENTS

Downloading and Installing the Software i

What is NOTION Conducting?
What Can You Do With This Curriculum? 1

Quick Start
Open a Score 2
Score Layouts 2
MIDI Keyboard Option 3
Perform a Score 3
Lose Your Place? 3
Quick Tour of NOTION Conducting 4

Play a Video
Select a Video 5
Operate a Video 5

Performance Mode
Perform a Score 6
Start at a Specific Location 6
Play a Score 7
Adjust Audio with the Mixer 7
Create a Customized Layout File 7

Edit Mode
Sidebar 8
Keyboard Shortcuts 8
Examples of Edits You Can Make 8

Customize Your View
Adjust Zoom 9
Change Page View 9

Fundamentals of Conducting
Pulse, Beat, and Meter 10
Grip the Baton 10
Beat Styles 11
Starting the Music 13
Expression 13

Showing an Effective Pulse; Beat Patterns in 2, 3, 4; Fermatas
Preparatory Exercise - Downbeats 14
Bach, O Grosser Gott von Macht 14
Sousa, The Thunderer - March 16
Smith, The Star-Spangled Banner 32

Controlling Tempo
Preparatory Exercise - Fluid Beats 38

        Ravel, Ma mère l'Oye - Pavane 38
        Ravel, Ma mère l'Oye - Petit Poucet 42

    Subdivision, Tempo Change
        Preparatory Exercise - Subdivision 54
        Beethoven, Symphony No. 1 - Movement I 54

    Variations in Beat Style
        Preparatory Exercise - Elided Beats 98
        Beethoven - Symphony No. 7 - Movement I 98
        Preparatory Exercise – Syncopation 124
        Holst, Second Suite for Band - Movement III 124
        Preparatory Exercise – Tempo Control 130
        Mozart, Die Zauberflöte - Overture 130

    Expressive Conducting
        Elgar, Serenade for Strings - Movement II 140
        Tchaikovsky, Romeo and Juliet Overture 144
        Wagner, Tristan und Isolde - Prelude.............................160
        Debussy, Prelude a l'après-midi d'un faune 168
        Puccini, La Bohème - Mi chiamano Mimi 176

    APPENDIX A – Glossary of Terms 188

    APPENDIX B – Dynamic and Articulation Marks 190

    APPENDIX C – Transposition...191

    APPENDIX D – Instruments and Clefs 193

Downloading and installing the Notion Conducting Software

Download:

1. Log-in, or create an account, at my.presonus.com

2. Click 'Register A Product' and choose product type (Software)

3. Enter the Product Key found with this book. Notion Conducting will now be registered to your account

4. Download the software installer from your my.presonus products area (either for Mac or Windows)

(And while you are there, why not download a free demo of the full notation version of Notion, or Studio One Prime, our free DAW?)

Install:

5. Once the software is completed, go to your Downloads folder and double click the file to start installation, and follow the on-screen instructions

WHAT IS NOTION CONDUCTING?

Conducting is the art of musical communication and coordination through meaningful gestures. Learning to conduct involves three requirements: a number of live musicians who can respond to the conductor's gestures, sufficient feedback to experience the musical result of the gestures, and a teacher who can devote full attention to helping each student. Ideally, an entire orchestra would be available for the conducting student. Since that is usually impossible, many conducting classes settle on a single pianist (usually the teacher), a small makeshift ensemble, or a CD for this purpose. The musical experience provided by one or a few instruments, however, is not equivalent to that of a full orchestra, nor does conducting a CD offer any direct communication with live human beings.

NOTION Conducting changes all that. Now you can conduct a live "orchestra" every time you go to class or study at home. This is the only teaching solution for conducting that combines music sampling technology, intuitive software, and a workbook built around a curriculum of standard orchestral literature.

With this virtual orchestra environment, teacher and students alike experience firsthand the challenges and rewards of studying conducting with a live ensemble – without the pressures of hiring an actual orchestra for rehearsals.

NOTION Conducting is also the first teaching tool that enables teachers to assign meaningful homework exercises for their class, and provides students a convenient way to practice and rehearse with a live ensemble practically anytime, anywhere.

This workbook contains:

- A brief guide to using this curriculum in a conducting class.
- A section of elementary instruction on conducting, including meter, baton grip, beat techniques, and expression.
- Conducting exercises and excerpts, arranged in order of difficulty, with explanatory notes on the specific conducting challenges of each score.
- Several appendices, including a glossary of terms, dynamic and articulation marks, transpositions of instruments, and typical clefs for instruments.
- A product key, to download the NOTION Conducting software, that includes score files for the excerpts in this workbook as well as a full collection of video lessons and performances of Dr. Jarrett and Dr. Oertel conducting the scores in this workbook.

What Can You Do With This Curriculum?

With NOTION Conducting you can:

- Conduct a virtual orchestra made up of fellow students, each controlling a portion of the orchestra in direct response to your gestures.
- Watch video lessons of conducting basics and performances of scores in this workbook being conducted. This valuable aid helps students at every level learn and master the nuances of conducting.
- Become thoroughly familiar with outstanding musical scores by master composers. You can single-out individual instruments and combinations to discover how they contribute to the overall orchestral effect.
- Develop strong rhythmic sight-reading skills. The ability to read rhythms is an essential component of a conductor's skill set.
- By muting one (or more) parts, you have the option of playing corresponding live instruments with a full orchestra accompanying you.
- Fashion your own musical interpretations. You can add, delete, or change tempo, dynamic, and articulation marks in the score to create different musical effects you can hear in playback.
- Learn to detect wrong notes and other score deviations set by the instructor.

QUICK START

Since most built-in computer speakers are not loud enough to generate effective orchestral sound, in a classroom setting it is best to use good-quality external speakers for each computer - check out the PreSonus Eris or Ceres speakers at your local music retailer.

Open a Score

1. Locate and open the **Conducting** application. On Windows, go to the **Start Menu** and look under **Programs**. On Mac, go to **Applications**.
   » The first score, the Preparatory Exercise - Downbeats, automatically opens.

2. Go to the Menu bar and click **File** and then click **Workbook Scores**.
   » A flyout menu of the scores in this workbook appears.

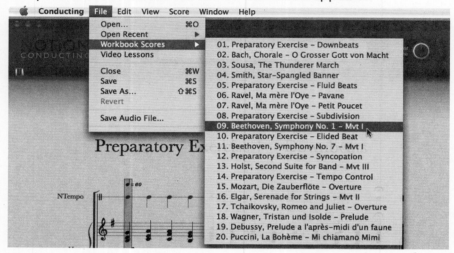

3. Click the score you want.
   » A new score replaces the exercise.

4. In the Menu bar, click **Score** and then select the layout you want this particular computer to play.
   » There are different layouts to choose from. See below for details.

5. You can now start performing the score with a standard computer keyboard or an external MIDI keyboard. See next page for a chart of shortcuts and MIDI keys you can use.

Score Layouts

NOTION Conducting can accommodate virtually any class size, from self-study to a lab of twenty or more. Each score comes with several layouts (available under the **Score** menu heading) to provide different instrumental groupings, depending on the size of the class.

· Full Score layout – shows and plays the full instrumentation. This is useful for individual study or for a class of only one or two students.

· Ensemble sections layout – shows and plays only single instrument families, such as Woodwinds, Brass, and so on. These enable students to hear and focus on individual sections.

· Conductor layouts – divide the orchestra into spatial slices according to typical orchestral seating. This is usually the most useful for classroom participation. Wherever possible, the computers should form a semicircle around the conductor:

	Orchestra	Band
Conductor Left	First Violins, Harp, and Percussion	Clarinets, Trumpets/Cornets
Conductor Left - Center	Second Violins, Flutes, Clarinets	Flutes, Oboe, Percussion, Bass Clarinets
Conductor Center - Right	Violas, Oboes, Bassoons, Horns, Trumpets, Trombones	Bassoons, Trombones, Tuba, String Bass
Conductor Right	Cellos, Basses, Tuba	Saxophones, Horns, Euphoniums

For large classes, it may be advisable to further subdivide the orchestra. This can be done in the Mixer, by clicking **Solo** for a single instrument or holding down SHIFT while clicking **Solo** for multiple instruments.

MIDI Keyboard Option

In addition to pressing keys on a standard computer keyboard to perform scores in NOTION Conducting, you can also use an external MIDI keyboard. If the MIDI device is velocity sensitive, you can control the computer's output volume by how hard you press the keys, providing an added dimension to your response to the conductor's gestures.

NOTE: If NOTION Conducting seems to either over-react or under-react to velocity changes as you perform, you can adjust sensitivity under or **File** > **Preferences** (Win) **Conducting** > **Preferences** (Mac).

Perform a Score

These quick-reference tables list the most commonly used operations to perform a score (you continuously control tempo by tapping). See **PERFORMANCE MODE** – starting on page 6 – for details. Before starting, ensure the **Perform** button is selected (it has a red border).

PLAYBACK

	Computer Keyboard	MIDI Keyboard
Perform	A, S, D, F, G, H, J, K, L, ;, or '	C4, D4, E4, F4, G4, A4, or B4
Pause	Q	D#3
Stop	ESC or SPACEBAR	C5 or any navigation key
Auto-Resume (software plays tempos marked in score)	R	G#4
Auto-Cruise (software continues with the tempo you set)	U	F#4

NAVIGATION

Move the green bar to...	Computer Keyboard	MIDI Keyboard
Place you last started	BACKSPACE (once)	A#3 (once)
Beginning	BACKSPACE (twice) or HOME	A#3 (twice)
Next measure	] or SHIFT + Right Arrow	D3
Previous measure	[or SHIFT + Left Arrow	C3
Next rehearsal mark	SHIFT +]	G#3
Previous rehearsal mark	SHIFT + [	F#3
Next beat/cutoff	Right Arrow	D#3
Previous beat	Left Arrow	C#3

Lose Your Place?

It happens: you discover you are no longer in sync with the rest of the ensemble. If this occurred while you were playing a musical instrument, you would stop and wait for the ensemble to reach a known landmark in the score and then resume playing. The same is true with tapping: you should *not* tap quickly through a series of notes to "catch up."

Instead, use any (or, usually, a mix of) navigation keyboard shortcuts/MIDI keys listed above. All your sounds stop when you press *any* of these keys, so you're immediately free to move the green playback marker to a known landmark in the score and begin tapping again when the ensemble reaches that spot.

NOTION Conducting provides many convenient features in the main window for performing in class.

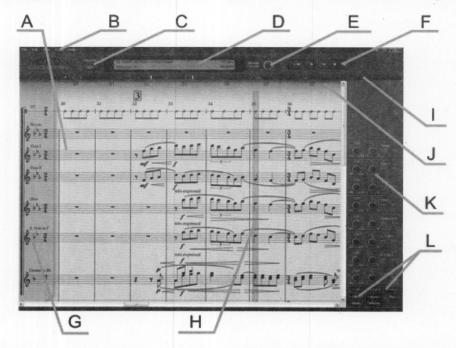

A: **Score area** – You view the score in this space. The score automatically moves as you perform or play through a file.

B: **Menu bar** – Provides convenient menu access to most features.

C: **Perform** and **Edit** buttons – Click **Perform** to perform scores (Performance mode). Click **Edit** to make any interpretation changes to the score (Edit mode).

D: **Performance display** – Updates you on current playback details, such as your current tempo (the bottom number in the picture to the right) compared to the written tempo (the upper number).

E: **Main volume** – Overall loudness control. All the way to the left is silence and all the way to the right is full output.

F: **Transport** – Buttons you click to control playback features during performance and editing. The important ones in Performance mode are:

- **Stop** ■ – Halts playback through the score at the current location of the green highlight bar (See letter H, below).

- **Rewind** ◄ – Click once to return to the location where you last started in the score. Click twice to return to the beginning.

- **Play** ► – In class, you control the tempo all during playback. But, for study, you have the option of clicking the Play button to have NOTION Conducting automatically play the score, using the notated tempos written in the score.

G: **Margin** – An overlay on top of the score that stays in place along the left side of the window that identifies the current instrument, clef, key signature, and time signature for each staff. This is a feature of **Continuous** view, the default page view (see **CUSTOMIZE YOUR VIEW** on page 9).

H: **Playback Marker** – A colorful semi-transparent bar that extends on the same beat through all staffs in the same system. This marks the current location in the score for playback. In Performance mode this will be green in color.

I: **Timeline** – A thin strip representing the measure numbers in the entire score. Thin silver lines in the timeline indicate the portion of the score you are currently viewing. A red line indicates the measure where the highlight bar is at the moment. You can click a measure number on the timeline to jump to another location in the score.

J: **Measure number bar** – A semi-transparent row that identifies measure numbers. This row automatically updates as you progress through the score.

K: **Mixer** – Individual panels that represent individual instruments (staffs) in the score. Each panel enables you to control the individual volume and pan (stereo placement) of an instrument. You can also solo or mute individual instruments. (More details about the Mixer appear on page 7.)

L: Buttons at the bottom of the Mixer area help you find the panel for a particular instrument (staff).

TIP: Under the **Help** menu heading are several tutorial scores to introduce you to the basic features of NOTION Conducting.

PLAY A VIDEO

Included in this edition of NOTION Conducting is an entire collection of conducting videos. Since conducting is an animated skill, full-motion video can be an invaluable tool for learning the nuances of the craft. Videos of the scores in this workbook and lessons on basic conducting concepts are included.

You can analyze how a professional conductor approached conducting a particular score while listening to the music. Or, you can soften (or turn off) the audio track, bring up the score in NOTION Conducting software, and tap through the piece, following the conductor from the standpoint of a musician in the orchestra.

Select a Video

1. Go to the Menu bar and select **File** > **Video Lessons**.
   » A new window opens with a menu of options.
2. Click your choice.
   » You view a menu of videos available.
3. Click your choice of video.
   » The video loads into the window and plays on its own.
4. When you place your cursor over the video you view playback controls (detailed below).
5. You can select another video on the menu or go to the links in the upper right to jump to the other menu or return to the initial menu screen.
6. When finished, simply close the window.

Operate a Video

A control panel appears when you hover your cursor anywhere over the video area.

A - Pause/Play

B - Stop

C - Progress bar. You can click anywhere on the bar to jump to that portion of the video.

D - Audio on/off

E - Audio volume

Set Audio

If you tap through the score while watching the conductor in the video, you can either:

· Set the video volume level lower so the video's playback is not as prominent as the NOTION Conducting audio, but you can still hear if you are not with the ensemble, or

· You can disable the audio of the video altogether, if you want to follow the conductor (without the video's audio cues).

PERFORMANCE MODE

Perform a Score

In Performance mode you control the musical rhythm (and, consequently, the tempo) while following the gestures of the conductor. Opening a NOTION Conducting score automatically places you in Performance mode. To switch out of Edit mode back to Performance mode – or whenever you are uncertain if you are in Performance mode or not – click the **Perform** button.

While in Performance mode, the green playback marker indicates the current playback position in the score. When you first open a score, this bar appears at the beginning.

To perform, go to your computer keyboard and tap *any* key on the row that starts with the letter "**A**" – or use the MIDI keyboard equivalents listed under **PERFORM A SCORE** on page 3. The faster you tap, the faster the tempo; the slower you tap, the slower the pace.

NTempo Staff

When you tap, you perform in accordance with the rhythm notated in the *NTempo staff*. This is the single-line staff with unpitched notes in a blue color.

Each time you tap, the cursor moves from one note in the NTempo staff to the next and you hear NOTION Conducting play whatever music lies between the two notes. Thus, you tap as if you were playing a percussion instrument, in accordance with the conductor's beat.

The notated rhythm in the NTempo staff usually consists of regular beats, but at key points it may also subdivide the beats so you can better control *rubato*. In the example (right), the NTempo line (the upper staff) matches the triplet figure in the ensemble. At this point, each tap covers a separate beat in the triplet so you can play the triplet straight, dramatically slow (or hurried), or syncopated, according to the conductor's lead.

It *is* possible to edit the NTempo rhythm. For details, see **Edit NTempo Staff** in Section 4 in the NOTION Conducting Help files.

Auto-Cruise

If a classroom situation calls for an extended steady tempo, you can set a pace and then tell NOTION Conducting to "cruise" at that speed. Tap until you establish a tempo you like, then tap the **U** key or F#4 on a MIDI keyboard. You can immediately regain control at any time simply by resuming normal Performance Mode tapping back on the "**A**" row.

Auto-Resume

You can switch from performing a score (you set tempos) to playing a score (tempo marks in the score set tempos) by pressing "R" – or G#4 on a MIDI keyboard.

Stop

To pause, press **Q**. To stop performing, press the SPACEBAR or ESC, or click the Stop button ▣ in the transport.

Start at a Specific Location

You don't have to always start at the beginning. To quickly move the playback marker to another location in the score you can use the keyboard shortcuts listed in the **Navigation** table under **Perform a Score** on page 3. Also helpful are these other methods:

- Go to the Timeline and click on a measure number.
- Use the Go To dialog. Press CTRL + G (Win) or ⌘ + G (Mac). Type either a measure number or rehearsal mark in the appropriate text box and click Go.

With either method, the playback marker jumps to that measure. You are ready to resume tapping.

Play a Score

To become better acquainted with a piece, you can *play* a score. Much like a CD, the software automatically plays the file by following the tempo marks written on the score.

- To start, press the SPACEBAR or the ▶ button in the upper right.
- To stop, press the SPACEBAR again, ESC, or the ■ button.
- To move the green highlight bar, you can use the navigation keys in the table on page 3.

Adjust Audio with the Mixer

The Mixer is actually a collection of different panels: each panel represents a different staff, identified by its instrument name. With panels you can control on a per-instrument basis:

- Gain (volume), with the left knob.
- Panning (the relative left-to-right position in stereo output), with the right knob.

 If you do not see the staff (instrument) you need, go to the buttons underneath the Mixer panels and click the musical section to which the instrument belongs (such as Brass or Strings; these buttons change with each score). If all the staves for this section do not fit on the Mixer in one viewing, you may need to click a green arrow button to access other panels.

To use a knob, click and drag an edge of the knob up or down. Or, if you prefer, double-click the knob, replace the current number in the temporary text box with the number you want an press ENTER. The middle (12:00 position) is considered 0.000. To the left you must prefix a number with a negative symbol (dash). To the right you need no symbol.

You can use the Mixer to solo and mute specific instruments. Go to a particular instrument's panel and click the **Solo** (green LED) or **Mute** (red LED) text. To solo or mute multiple instruments, hold down SHIFT while clicking the corresponding **Solo** or **Mute** texts.

For more details about using the Mixer, refer to **The Mixer** in Section 3 of The NOTION Conducting Help files.

Create a Customized Layout File

As mentioned in **Quick Start**, there are pre-determined layouts in each score (under the **Score** menu) that will limit what you see on your screen and hear while performing/playing a score. If none of these layouts addresses a need you have, you can use solo or mute in the Mixer, as discussed above. Another option is to create a file with your own customized layout using one or more instruments you select. This way, the next time you open this file you see your custom layout (and Mixer settings).

1. Go to the Menu bar and select **Score > Show/Hide Staffs**.
   » A dialog box opens with a list of all the staffs (instruments) in the score.
2. Select the parts you want shown and de-select the ones you want hidden.
3. Click the **OK** button.
   » You view in the score area only the part(s) you selected.
4. If you want only selected instrument(s) to play, click **Solo** in the Mixer for one instrument or hold down SHIFT and click **Solo** for multiple instruments.
5. To create your own version of the file with this exact setup, do a Save As. Either:
   – Go to the Menu bar and select **File > Save As**, or
   – Press CTRL + SHIFT + s (Win) or ⌘ + SHIFT + s (Mac).
   – Specify a name for the file and (if you want) a different hard drive location and click **Save**.
6. To open this file, select **File > Open** in the Menu bar, or go to the operating system and double-click the file.

Edit Mode

You can edit, add, or delete certain score markings to create your own interpretation. To access editing features, you have to work in Edit mode. This is easy to do: simply click the Edit button in the upper left.

Aside from the ability to edit certain score markings, Edit mode also:

- Switches the playback marker from a green to a light gray to indicate that you are in Edit mode. When you click on a staff to select it, a bright yellow box appears at that location to show where you clicked and a light gray highlight bar extends at that beat to all other staffs in the system.
- Introduces a new cursor type called the Music Cursor. This editing cursor appears only in the score area, and only when you are in Edit mode. You place a symbol (such as a dynamic mark) in the Music Cursor to add it to the score.
- Supports a modified form of tapping. Since editing is generally completed outside of class, the most common form of playback in Edit mode is playing a score: using the notated tempo marks. Conveniently, the SPACEBAR both starts and stops this type of playback (or you can use the Play and Stop buttons in the Transport). However, you are perfectly free to tap in Edit mode, but there are two major changes.
  - To be able to tap, you have to click where you want to start and then click the ▶ button. The light gray playback marker changes to green and you can tap as you do in Performance mode.
  - Stopping (with the Stop button, ESC, or SPACEBAR) takes you immediately back to Edit mode. You see the green playback marker change to a light gray color so you can immediately make an edit.

Sidebar

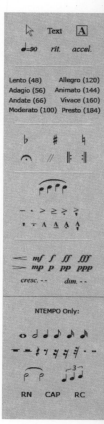

In the Sidebar appear commonly used score symbols you can click to add to a score. This panel takes the place of the Mixer at the right side of the window.

To view, go to the Menu bar and click **View**. Then click **Show Sidebar**. Although you can see the Sidebar in Performance mode, it is accessible for editing only in Edit mode.

To use, be in Edit mode and click any symbol. Notice that your cursor now is a Music Cursor: in the Score area it displays a representation of that symbol in a blue color. Alternately, you can press shortcut keys on your computer keyboard to select a symbol.

See **Add Marks** (at bottom of this page) for an example of how to add a symbol that is in your Music Cursor to the score.

Keyboard Shortcuts

When you are in Edit mode (and not tapping) the keys on the computer keyboard are set for editing shortcuts instead of performing a score. For example, an "F" key that can be used for tapping in Performance mode will instead place a forte dynamic mark in your Music Cursor. The NOTION Conducting Help system details all the various shortcuts available.

Included with this workbook is a *Quick Reference Guide* that provides a summary of the shortcuts available in NOTION Conducting.

Examples of Edits You Can Make

You cannot delete or add essential score markings, such as notes, rests, or measures. But you are able to edit markings such as dynamics, articulations, fermatas, caesuras, and more.

Add Marks

As an example, here are the steps to place *staccato* marks on certain notes you select:

1. To clear your cursor, press ESC once.
2. Press the "1" key once.
   » You view a small dot in a blue color on your cursor. This is a *staccato* mark. If you accidentally press the 1 key more than once, keep pressing until you view a dot again.

3. Position your cursor at the head of a note you want to alter. Either click your mouse or press ENTER. Repeat this on any number of other notes you want.
» These notes now have *staccato* marks. NOTION Conducting will interpret and play the *staccato* articulation correctly in playback.

4. To save your interpretation in a different file, do a **Save As**.

Delete Marks

To delete marks, your cursor must be a Pointer. Press ESC if the cursor displays any symbol. Then:

· Click a single mark in the score so it turns blue, or

· To select multiple marks, hold down the SHIFT key as you click. The marks turn blue in color to show they are selected.

Then press DELETE.

Edit Marks

Some marks, such as a tempo mark or fermata, can be edited if you double click them in the score. A temporary text box appears for you to enter a change. Then either press ENTER or click anywhere in the score area.

CUSTOMIZE YOUR VIEW

Adjust Zoom

To quickly jump from one preset zoom level to the next:

	Windows shortcut	*Mac shortcut*	*Menu bar*
Zoom in	CTRL + =	⌘ + =	**View > Zoom In**
Zoom out	CTRL + -	⌘ + -	**View > Zoom Out**

If your mouse has a scroll wheel, you can hold down CTRL (PC) or ⌘ (Mac) as you roll the wheel away from you (zoom in) or towards you (zoom out).

You also have the option of entering a percentage size.

1. Open a **Zoom To** dialog box, either by:
   – Going to the Menu bar and selecting **View > Zoom To**, or
   – Pressing CTRL + SHIFT + = (PC) or ⌘ + SHIFT + = (Mac).

2. Enter a percentage in the text box. Actual size is 100.

3. Click the **OK** button.

Change Page View

NOTION Conducting provides two main ways of viewing each score. When you go to the Menu bar and click **View**, the two options at the top are:

· **Continuous** – This default view is well-suited for most scores. This uninterrupted scroll moves the playback marker through the score as you play – with no page breaks. At the far left appears a margin: an overlay on top of the score that identifies each staff's instrument abbreviation (in a red color), current clef, time signature, and key signature.

· **Across** – This more traditional "page" look moves the score as you play, but with visible page breaks. Instrument abbreviations, clefs, and time/key signatures always appear at the left edge of a new "page" where you expect to find them on published scores.

Fundamentals of Conducting

The majority of the following information can be viewed in NOTION Conducting videos, under **Lessons**.

Pulse, Beat, and Meter

Pulse is a regularly recurring unit of musical time. Large pulses can be broken down into combinations of shorter pulses. The particular relationship among larger and shorter pulses within a given musical episode is called its metric structure, or *meter*.

There are two distinct meanings for the musical term *beat*. From a listener's standpoint, beat is the pulse unit that is most prominent within a metric structure. Usually this will be the pulse that one intuitively taps while listening to music. For the conductor and ensemble however, beat is the particular level of pulse the conductor chooses to mark. Although the conductor's beat may often correspond to the intuitive musical beat, there may be practical reasons why this may not always be the case.

Meter is indicated by meter signatures (more commonly referred to as time signatures). Time signatures always indicate how many (upper figure) of a given note value (lower figure) are found in a bar.

In addition, if the upper figure is a power of 2 (e.g., 2, 4, 8, 16), the meter is usually called *simple*. In simple meters, the pulse represented by the lower figure combines in twos to form the next higher pulse.

If the upper figure of a meter signature is a multiple of 3 (e.g., 3, 6, 9, 12, 15), the meter is called compound. In compound meters, the pulse represented by the lower figure combines in threes to form the next higher pulse.

 Time signatures with the upper figure of 5, 7, 10, 11, and so on, indicate irregular groupings of the pulse represented by the lower figure. Thus, a signature of 7/16 indicates that a bar contains seven sixteenth-notes, which can be combined into larger pulses as 2-2-3 (as in the example to the left), 2-3-2 or 3-2-2. Modern composers have been known to create irregular beats within 8/8 or 9/8.

Depending on the tempo, a conductor will normally choose to beat either the pulse represented by the lower number of the time signature, or the pulse of the next higher metric level. For example, a 6/8 meter may be beaten in six or in two, while a 4/8 may be beaten in four or in two. In the case of irregular groupings, this may result in beats of unequal length. The 7/16 example above may be beaten in three, with the third beat being one sixteenth longer than the other two beats. More often than not, the conductor's beat will represent either quarter-note or dotted-quarter-note durations, but there are many exceptions to this rule, particularly in slower tempos. The conductor should always let the ensemble know either the beat value itself or the number of beats in a bar.

The way in which eighth and sixteenth notes are grouped into beams usually reflects the composer's metric intentions. Thus a grouping of eighths into 3-3-2 within a 4/4 bar may indicate a meter of three irregular beats, rather than the usual four, particularly if other note and rest values indicate the 3-3-2 pattern. Such metric organizations are often expressed in the time signature. A few examples follow:

 Indicates a three-beat pattern with two beats consisting of three eighth notes and one beat consisting of two eighth notes.

 Indicates a two-beat pattern with one beat consisting of three eighth notes and one consisting of two eighth notes.

Grip the Baton

The basic purpose of the baton is to lengthen the arm and magnify movement of the wrist. If the wrist is not employed as an expressive element, there is little need for a baton. In order to gain maximum wrist flexibility, the baton should be held between the thumb and forefinger, with the thumb pointing in the same direction as the baton. If the baton has a ball grip, the other fingers can then close around the ball, enabling the baton to be held securely. Never hold the baton in a fist grip (perpendicular to the direction of the thumb), as it can inflict severe damage to the face or throat in moments of musical excitement. It should be possible to raise and lower the baton, and to describe a circle with the baton, through movement of the wrist alone. The grip on the baton should be relaxed, but firm enough to maintain control.

Prepared Beat

Consider the characteristics of a ball as it is tossed up into the air and falls to the ground. When the ball is thrown up, the speed of the ball slows as it reaches the maximum height allowed by gravity. Once at its peak, gravity pulls it back down in a movement that is very familiar and predictable for human beings.

The prepared beat is one in which a similar motion of the baton enables the players to anticipate the beat point with accuracy. Three steps are involved in effectively delivering a prepared beat:

1. The beat point (or horizontal plane where the sound is to occur) is indicated by the position of the tip of the baton prior to beginning the preparation.
2. The preparation is formed by lifting the baton upwards away from the beat point.
3. The beat itself is delivered by dropping the baton back to the beat point in a natural, relaxed fall, responding to the pull of gravity.

The baton should neither be thrust downward, nor inhibited due to tension in the wrist or arm. It should arrive at the beat point in a position parallel to the floor, not pointing downward. The movement away from and back to the beat point is achieved most naturally through lifting and dropping the wrist. In fact, showing the palm of the hand when lifting the wrist is a gesture always interpreted by players as indicating a preparation. Using the wrist and gravity to control preparation and beat not only frees the arm for other expressive purposes, it also enables the conductor to achieve control without becoming tired.

The purpose of the prepared beat is to ensure accuracy of attack at the beat point itself. Since a sound is to begin at the beat point, a player cannot wait until he or she sees the actual beat point before beginning the physical sound-producing process. Therefore, accuracy of attack does not depend on reaching the beat point itself, but rather on the predictability with which the beat point is approached. Although it may feel to the conductor as if the beat point "causes" the sound, the fact is that the process of making the sound has already begun by the time the beat point is reached.

When using the prepared beat, the first beat of a bar, or downbeat, always drops from directly above the beat point.

The last beat of a bar (assuming there is more than one beat in the bar) drops slantwise from the right. Following each beat, the baton rises in a direction either straight up or opposite that of the next beat point. Each beat motion prepares the next. In a four-beat bar, for example, the baton rebounds to the right following the initial downbeat, then drops to the left for the second beat. Then it rebounds up and drops again to the right for the third beat. For the fourth beat, it rises and drops leftward (back to the middle position). From there it rises directly upward in preparation for the downbeat of the next bar. Note that the last beat of the bar, if it is a prepared beat, is always downward to the middle position, never upward. The upward motion following the last beat of a bar is actually the beginning of the preparation for the next downbeat.

The conductor may choose to place the beat at different points along the beat plane in order to give greatest clarity to the beat pattern, or he or she may choose to place all beats at the same point in order to achieve the greatest degree of predictability. The former practice is useful in situations involving *rubato*, fermatas, and mixed meters to make the beat pattern perfectly clear. The latter practice is employed when utmost precision of attack at the beat point is desired.

As long as musical events occur on the beat, with little or no subdivision between beats, fermatas and changing tempos can be easily controlled by slowing or speeding up the preparations. If greater control over subdivision between beats during a ritardando is necessary, the conductor must either subdivide the beat (which, in effect, means adding extra beats within the bar) or adopt the circular beat style described next.

Circular Beat

The circular beat is a controlled circular movement from one beat point to the next, usually involving both arm and wrist. Because the pathway of a circle is more predictable than a straight line, it is possible to indicate by the motion of the baton through a circular path how long it will take to return to the beat point. Players can judge where their subdivisions would occur by estimating the baton's position within the circular path. The circular motion can be completely regular in speed, as when indicating the sudden onset of a new tempo, or it can slow down during the circle, indicating ritardando within the beat. In the latter case, it is generally advisable to let the wrist drop to the beat point at the last moment, in order to ensure a good attack. A sudden *ritardando* or *ritenuto* is best indicated by beginning the circle with the tip of the baton lowered. This lets the players know immediately that the next beat will be delayed.

The circular beat is difficult to master and always contains an element of danger. It should be used with caution, and delivered in such a way as to ensure full attention on the part of the ensemble.

Elided Beat

Often there is no musical event on a particular beat requiring preparation. For example, in a four-beat 4/4 bar, the ensemble rhythm may consist of quarter-half-quarter. In such a case, it is better not to prepare the third beat, since there is no need, and such preparation might inadvertently cause someone to play at the wrong time. Instead, the baton stops at the beat point of the second beat, and then moves directly to that of the third beat in a horizontal motion of the arm to the right without raising the wrist. As soon as the third beat area is reached, the wrist lifts the baton to begin preparation for the fourth beat. In this way, the entire third beat becomes a smooth preparation for the fourth beat.

Downbeats cannot be elided. In cases where the entire ensemble plays only on the downbeat or where there is a full bar rest for the entire ensemble, only the downbeat need be given, with all the other beats in the bar elided.

Stop Beat

Although sometimes called the "staccato" beat, use of the stop beat is not necessarily limited to *staccato* passages. In this beat style, the baton moves in a straight line as quickly as possible to each beat point and stops at the beat point until time for the next beat. No preparations are given for beats. The first beat of the bar is always directly downward, and the last beat is always upward, with its beat point directly above the point of the first beat. The beat is made with the arm, not the wrist. In fact, the wrist actually moves in contrary motion to the arm, in order to maintain the same viewing angle of the baton throughout the beat pattern.

The stop beat is used in situations where the conductor must maintain a steady, metronomic tempo while the ensemble executes subdivisions of the beat. Here, the most important musical consideration is the accuracy of events lying between beats. Since there are no preparations, the momentum of these events must lead the players into the next beat. By indicating only the onset of each pulse, the conductor forces the players to follow their own inner subdivision of the beat. By avoiding preparations, the conductor indicates that the tempo is "rock steady." When giving the stop beat, it is important not to move the baton until all subdivisions of a beat have been executed. Letting the baton wander between beats suggests possible *rubato*, which can mislead the players into mistrusting their own inner subdivision of the beat.

Dead or "Vacant" Beat

The dead beat is a conducting gesture or beat that cannot be played upon. The dead beat can be described as a vacant beat devoid of predictable and playable characteristics. It is made by dropping the wrist in a limp manner, so that the tip of the baton points downward. This is useful when marking time for the ensemble during empty bars, as during a recitative or passage for soloist alone.

Starting the Music

Pop music performers sometimes start things off by audibly counting out two full measures. This is part of the "show," and is in no way necessary. It should always be possible to indicate tempo visually with a single beat preparation. Giving more than one beat is usually not only superfluous, but can cause confusion. In theory, it is not even necessary for an ensemble to know the tempo prior to the starting beat unless there are rhythmic subdivisions to be played between the first and second beats.

The initial preparation for an ensemble depends on the beat style to be employed. If the prepared beat is used, the preparation for the first attack will be exactly like a normal preparation for that beat. If the initial tempo is critical, the wrist should make a slight dip to mark the beat point of the previous beat before beginning the preparation for the starting beat. For example, if the music is to start on the fourth beat of the bar, the wrist should mark the beat point of the third beat, followed immediately by a normal preparation for the fourth beat.

If the stop beat is to be employed for the starting beat (only if the music begins on a subdivision after the beat), tempo must be indicated with a stop beat on the beat which precedes the starting beat. For example, if the music begins after the second beat of a three-beat bar, the conductor must begin by moving the stick suddenly, without preparation, downward to a stop beat on the downbeat, then likewise to the right, to a stop beat on the second beat. The illustration to the right is an example of this situation.

Setting a tempo always requires the clear visual indication of two points in time, the first of which is the point of the beat prior the starting beat, and the second of which is the point of the starting beat itself.

Expression

Music both suggests and demands energy. Sometimes the conductor needs to indicate the kind of energy the music symbolizes. More often he or she needs to indicate the kind of energy and control demanded of the player, which may not always be the same thing. For example, playing softly generally requires more energy and control than playing at a moderate dynamic, although soft music usually symbolizes less energy. Through pantomime, the conductor can communicate to the players the kind of energy, control, or concentration needed at a given moment.

This is one of the most important aspects of successful conducting, and one of the hardest to develop.

The expressive conductor uses pantomime to create imaginary musical entities, which he or she can push and pull upon, stretch or compress, give energy to and take energy away from. Sometimes these imaginary entities are embodied in the players themselves, as the representatives of the sounds they produce. Thus the conductor may pull directly at the oboe soloist to invoke a louder sound, or push against the entire string section to quiet them down. At other times, he or she may raise the arms in such a way as to lift a heavy weight, to suggest a crescendo. Sometimes the conductor may drag the baton in such a way as to suggest resistance, indicating a slowing of tempo. Often the amount of energy expressed by the beat itself connotes musical energy. (This does not necessarily mean that loud music should have a large beat, or soft music should have a small beat. Great energy can be expressed in a small beat, and softness can be expressed in a large beat. In fact, beat size generally has more to do with control of tempo than with dynamics.)

A conductor who breathes with the music, and who amplifies the act of breathing through gestures, will elicit an empathetic expressive response from the ensemble, particularly singers and wind players. In fact, the entire technique of conducting can be understood as a way of formalizing and amplifying the breathing process. The essential act of breathing – the intake and exhaling of air – is directly reflected in the lifting and dropping of the baton while executing a prepared beat.

Finally, it should be kept in mind that ALL signals to an ensemble must be indicated prior to the actual event they are intended to elicit. For example, a forte attack requires a forte preparation. More pressure is needed to play loudly, and the body must prepare itself ahead of time for such effort. This kind of preparation comes naturally to a conductor whose own breathing mirrors the music, and whose gestures are motivated by the musical flow.

Conductors must master the art of non-verbal communication through practiced beats and gestures. Every movement, gesture, and beat from the conductor must have a purpose. Practice and prepare for each purpose and clear conducting will result.

CONDUCTING SCORES

Showing an Effective Pulse; Beat Patterns in 2, 3, 4; Fermatas

Preparatory Exercise - Downbeats

This is an exercise in giving clear prepared beats, insuring precision of attack at the beat point. No beat pattern is necessary, as all beats can be downbeats. The important thing is to focus on achieving a unison attack on each chord, while varying the tempo from beat to beat.

Each beat should be given by raising the tip of the baton with the wrist, then letting the baton fall naturally into a position parallel to the floor. Bear in mind that what the players will be reacting to is not the actual beat point itself, but the predictability of the fall of the baton into that point.

Bach, O Grosser Gott von Macht

The primary goal of this conducting exercise is to develop a clear prepared beat. Musical events in the chorale are limited primarily to one note per beat, although there are some instances of two notes per beat. The student should concentrate on achieving a simultaneous attack from the players at each beat.

Although the student should have in mind the pattern for a four beat, the pattern is initially less important in this exercise than is the clarity of the beat itself. Once mastered, the beat should be incorporated into the four pattern. Note that the preparation for each of the four beats should begin at the beat level, and that the beat itself is always a downward falling of the baton. Normally, beats one and four should both land in the middle of the beat level line, with beat two to the left and beat three to the right. For utmost clarity, however, all beats may be placed in the same central position, although approached from different directions.

The fermatas in this example are all followed by a rest. There is no need for a special cutoff. Simply pause the baton at the second beat of each fermata, then prepare and execute the next beat (the rest) as if it were a musical event. Since each fermata occurs on a half note, there is no need to prepare its second beat (no new musical event occurs within the half-note duration). Use the elided beat in this case. Finally, since the last note takes up an entire bar, there is no need to beat out the four pattern. Cut off the last note simply by giving another downbeat.

It is not necessary to indicate tempo through a preparatory beat at the beginning of the chorale, since the first beat is not subdivided. Note, however, that since the chorale begins on the fourth beat, its preparation must be made from the right, as if coming from the third beat of the bar.

"O Grosser Gott von Macht" BWV

J.S. Bach

Sousa, The Thunderer - March

This is a typical Sousa march, to be conducted in 2. The tempo should remain consistent throughout. Some sudden dynamic changes are involved: for example, the overall dynamic drop from *ff* to *mf* at the fifth bar, and again at bar 69. This can be indicated by a cautionary signal from the left hand, coinciding with a smaller upbeat of the baton. Similarly, the sudden *ff* on the second beat of bar 19 can be indicated in advance by the rebound from the downbeat.

As long as the ensemble maintains a steady tempo and no special conducting gesture is called for, it is wise to avoid overly conducting. A simple "twist" of the wrist between beats can suffice to keep things going, while making any special gestures more effective, by contrast.

Note: For optimal playback of this score please refer to recommended operating system requirements.

The Thunderer
March

John Philip Sousa

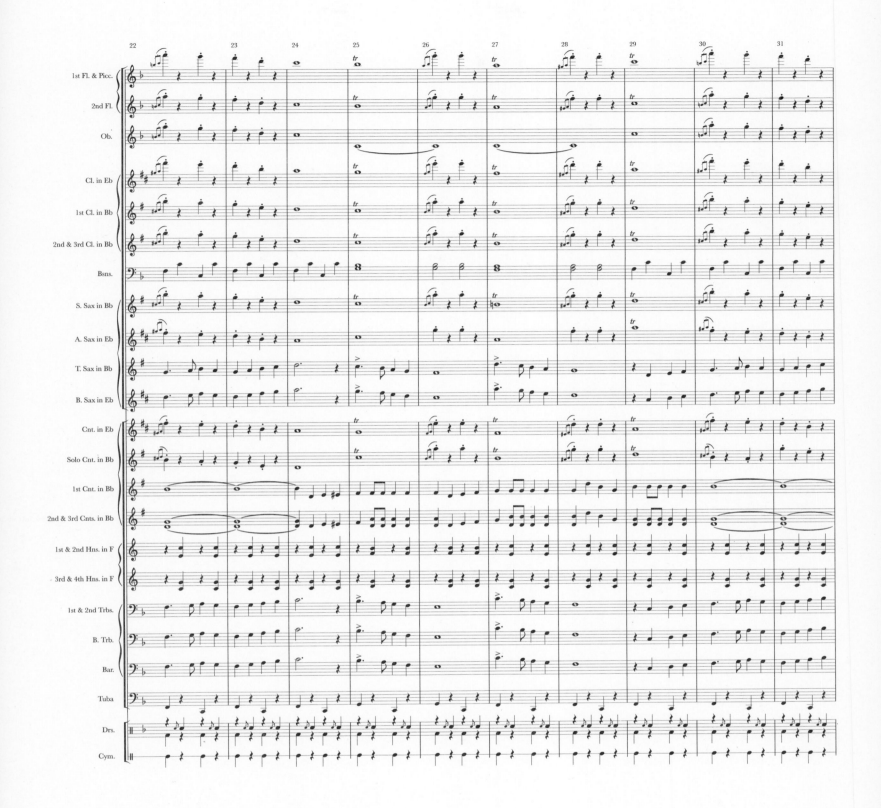

19

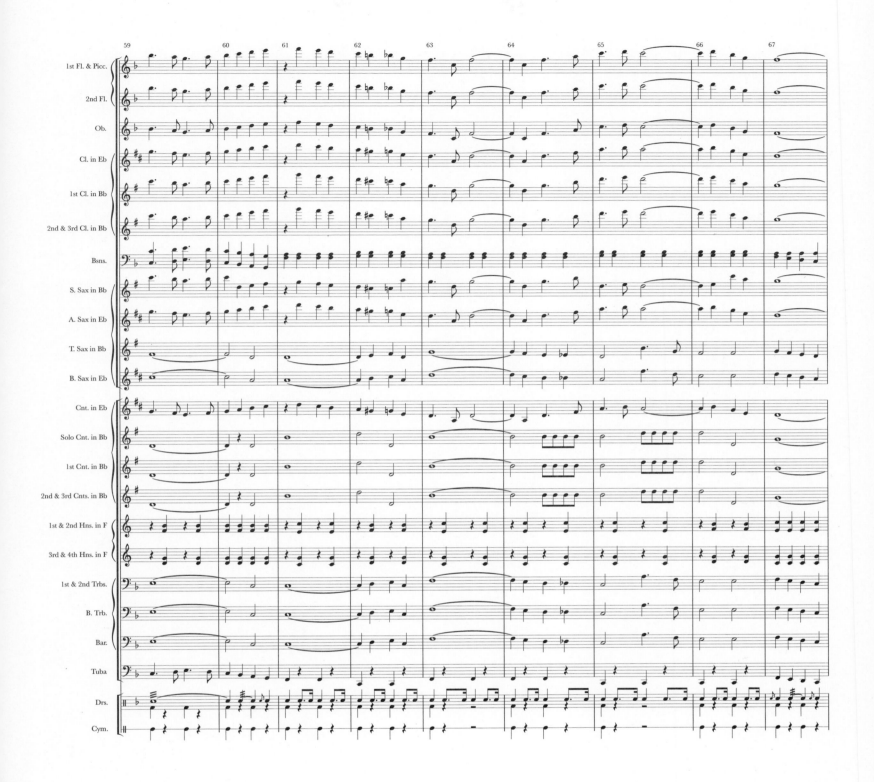

25

26

28

29

Smith, The Star-Spangled Banner

The fermata that occurs in bar 31 is different from those in the Bach Chorale, all of which occur before a rest. This one is best conducted by moving the baton slowly toward the right (to indicate beat 2), then quickly moving down toward the center (beat 3), ending with a "cutting" motion to the right. This is then followed by a new preparation and a repeat of beat 3 to bring the orchestra back in.

The Star-Spangled Banner

arr. Jack Jarrett

33

Controlling Tempo

Preparatory Exercise - Fluid Beats

This is an exercise in controlling tempo through the rise of the baton between beats. Try to telegraph when the next beat will fall by the way the baton rises from each beat. Slowing down can be indicated by dropping the tip of the baton as it rises, as if it had suddenly become heavier. Speeding up can be indicated by a quick rise, as if the baton were weightless. Don't expect perfection yet. This is a difficult thing to master.

Ravel, Ma mère l'Oye - Pavane

Unlike the Bach Chorale, this example consists primariliy of two notes per beat. The student should concentrate on achieving a fluid movement between beats, with the baton staying constantly in motion. The baton should bounce lightly from the beat point into the preparation for the next beat. Subtle tempo control is possible by varying the speed of the preparation. This takes some control, and should be the focus of the student's attention. The movement upward away from the beat should immediately signal any change in tempo, so that players can correctly anticipate when the next beat will occur. The student should experiment with creating a rallentando in bar 12, followed by a return to tempo in the following bar; without resorting to subdivision.

The preparation for the first beat should clearly indicate the tempo, since the first beat is to be subdivided by the flute. This can be achieved by a very slight snap of the wrist at the beat level, followed by the upward preparation for the first beat.

Ma mère l'Oye

Pavane

Maurice Ravel

Ravel, Ma mère L'Oye - Petit Poucet

Although similar to the previous Pavane, this example confronts the student with changing meters. In such situations, it is often advisable to exaggerate the beat pattern somewhat for the sake of clarity. Note that the 5/4 bars are best conducted as 3+2. This is achieved by placing beats 2 and 3 in the same direction, with beat 3 farther to the left than beat 2.

The last two beats of the next-to-last bar may be subdivided to achieve the indicated *rallentando*. This is done by repeating the fourth and fifth beats, bouncing in place with a motion clearly indicating preparation in the same direction as the primary beats.

Since the first beat of the example requires subdivision from the players, it is necessary to indicate the tempo in the preparation.

Ma mère l'Oye

Petit Poucet

Maurice Ravel

47

Subdivision, Tempo Change

Preparatory Exercise - Subdivision

This is an exercise in subdivision. While beating eighth notes, try varying the tempo in expressive ways. The same techniques for slowing down or speeding up should be employed as in the previous exercise, but in the context of a subdivided beat.

Beethoven, Symphony No. 1 - Movement 1

Since the first beat is not subdivided, it is not necessary to indicate the tempo prior to that beat, nor is it necessary to prepare the second beat of the first bar, since no new musical event occurs at that point. Use the elided beat instead. The baton should drop quickly into the third beat, to ensure simultaneity from the players.

At measure 4 the violins begin a melody in eighths and sixteenths. The student may wish to employ a subtle "stop-and-go" subdivision during the sixteenth-note passages. This involves stopping the baton at a primary beat point, then starting the preparation for the next beat on the following eighth – in effect separating the beat from the preparation by an eighth-note duration.

There are two ways to interpret the last four notes of measure 12. One is to continue to the end of the bar, as notated, in the current tempo, beginning the Allegro only in the next bar. The other is to treat these four thirty-second notes as sixteenths in the new tempo. This requires conducting the last two eighths of measure twelve as quarter-note preparations to the new tempo, using "stop" beats.

Symphony No. 1

Movement 1

Ludwig van Beethoven

94

Variations in Beat Style

Preparatory Exercise - Elided Beats

This is an exercise in varying the beat to fit the musical rhythm. Some beats should be elided, others subdivided.

Beethoven, Symphony No. 7 - Movement I

Several new challenges are found in this example. Although in 4/4, there is no need to prepare beats 2 and 4 in the first three bars, since no new musical events occur at those points. Clearly, there should be an indication of greater energy at the beginnings of the first, third and fifth bars. This is achieved through a larger preparation. There is no need to prepare the tempo before the first bar, since no subdivision occurs on the first beat.

At bar 9 a sequence of sixteenth notes begins. These are too fast to conduct separately or to control through subdivision. To achieve uniformity it is necessary for the conductor to first establish the tempo, and then to signal the players that they must subdivide the beat on their own. Preparations, although extremely useful for controlling rubato, can be distracting to players intent on holding a steady tempo while subdividing. The conductor, therefore, must give only the beat in metronomic fashion, without preparations. The "stop" beat should be employed for this reason.

For maximum clarity, the baton should remain parallel to the floor when giving a "stop" beat. This requires that the wrist compensate for the movement of the arm, particularly at the last beat of the bar, when the baton is raised. Lifting the tip of the baton suggests a preparation, and can confuse the players into thinking that the tempo is changing. Proper mastery of the "stop" beat technique is an important key to effective conducting.

At rehearsal letter D, the beat should be in 2. This tempo must be prepared in the last two eighths of the preceding bar.

Symphony No. 7

Movement 1

Ludwig van Beethoven

Preparatory Exercise - Syncopation

This is an exercise in maintaining a syncopated response to a steady beat. The conductor must maintain the tempo and not be distracted by sluggishness on the part of the players. If the players begin to lag behind the beat, the conductor must respond by being even more precise and energetic, not by giving in to the players' tempo. (See the comments below concerning the stop beat before attempting this exercise.)

Holst, Second Suite for Band - Movement III

This is an excellent exercise in using the stop beat to insure precision in syncopated rhythms. Although what the audience hears during the first bar is "Ta-Ta-Ta-ta-ta-ta," what the players must feel internally is "(OOM)-Ta-(OOM)-Ta-(OOM)-Ta-ta-ta-ta." The conductor must provide the "(OOM)"'s for the players, by giving quick, energetic pulses, while at the same time avoiding intervening motions that might detract from the visual clarity of the beats.

To begin, give the upbeat by quickly and vigorously raising the baton upward to a stopped position. The baton must stop in such a way as to indicate a clear ictus. For this reason, it is better to keep the baton parallel to the floor, rather than raising the tip and pointing the baton upward – a gesture that is normally interpreted as a "get ready" for something to come. In this case, what is important is the upbeat itself, since it, together with the downbeat to follow, must establish the tempo precisely.

Similarly, the first three beats of the opening bar itself must be clear stops, exactly in time. These are the "OOM"'s that allow the players to subdivide with full confidence. The same technique should be employed for every syncopated rhythm throughout the composition.

Note: For optimal playback of this score please refer to recommended operating system requirements.

Second Suite for Band

Movement III

Gustav Holst

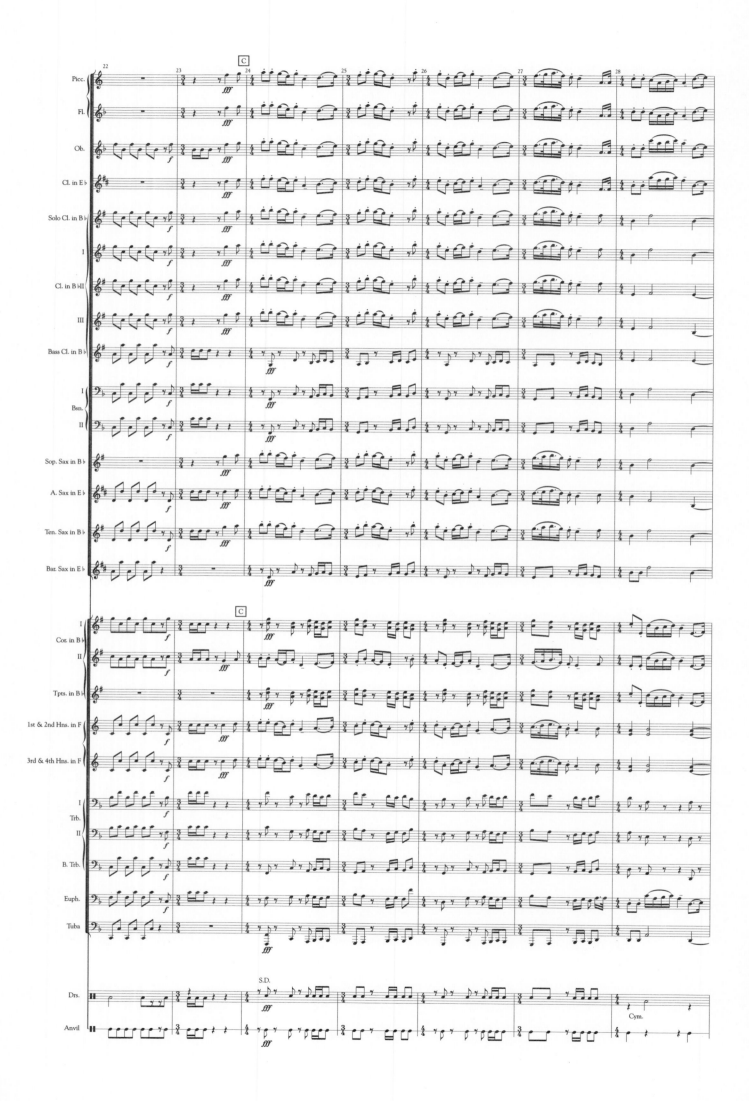

29
30
31
32
33
Picc.
Fl.
Ob.
Cl. in E♭
Solo Cl. in B♭
I
Cl. in B♭
II
III
Bass Cl. in B♭
I
Bsn.
II
Sop. Sax in B♭
A. Sax in E♭
Ten. Sax in B♭
Bar. Sax in E♭
I
Cor. in B♭
II
Tpts. in B♭
1st & 2nd Hns. in F
3rd & 4th Hns. in F
a2
I
Trb.
II
B. Trb.
Euph.
Tuba
Drs.
Cym.
Anvil

Preparatory Exercise - Tempo Control

This is an exercise in controlling a ritardando entirely within a single beat. Each of the triplet entrances below should be slower than the preceding one. Control is achieved through the upward motion of the baton during the triplet figure.

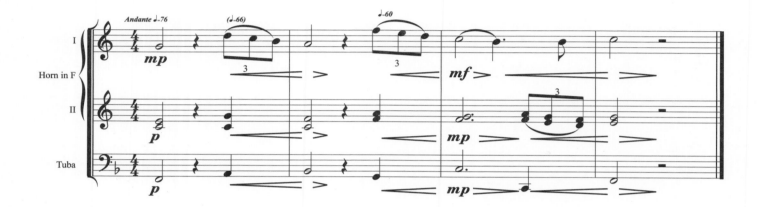

Mozart, Die Zauberflöte - Overture

The first three bars are especially tricky. There are several possible ways to conduct the sixteenth-note upbeats. The simplest method is "dictation," where the student conducts the notes directly, using a quick gesture aimed forward toward the players. The triplet thirty-second notes at the end of bar 3 are normally interpreted as slower than their actual notated value. After indicating the start of the three-note figure, it is necessary to have a clear, predictable, rising preparation movement toward the next downbeat, indicating the amount of time that is to be filled while performing the figure. At the end of bar 15 it is necessary to give an upbeat preparation for the new tempo. This preparation should be a "stop" beat equal in length to the coming half-note pulse. The ensuing Allegro is conducted in 2.

Die Zauberflöte
Overture

Wolfgang Amadeus Mozart

Elgar, Seranade for Strings - Movement II

This example contains both on-the-beat and within-the-beat events, in an expressive rubato context. Especially tricky is bar 8, where a broad second beat is needed to keep the triplet sixteenths from being rushed. Bar 16 calls for almost non-existent second, third and fourth beats, so as not to bring about an early entrance at the next bar. Dynamics are important throughout, particularly at the "inverted" (pianissimo) climax at bar 25, which should be approached with a subtle *rallentando*.

Serenade for Strings
Movement II

Edward Elgar

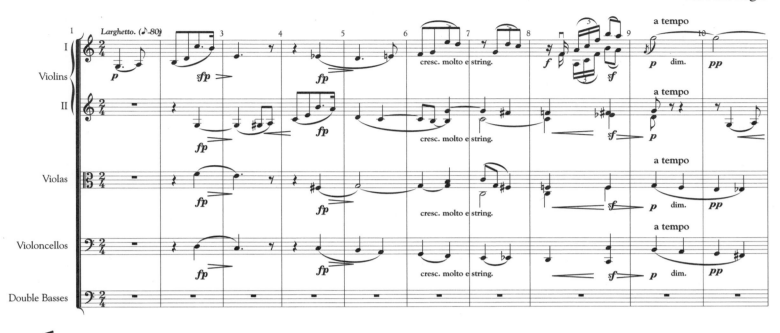

Tchaikovsky, Romeo and Juliet Overture

The opening section can be conducted in either 2 or 4. If in 4, there is no need to prepare the second beat of the half-note events in the first 20 bars. The pizzicato notes beginning at bar 38 require very clear beat preparations. An accelerando is required between bars 104 and the ensuing "Allegro giusto."

Romeo and Juliet Overture

Pitor Ilyich Tchaikovsky

152

157

Wagner, Tristan und Isolde - Prelude

This is an example of music in which little or no inner pulse is evident in the music itself. The first few bars consist of large-scale musical gestures, whose effect is created primarily through harmonic tension and dynamic rise and fall, rather than through an inner pulse. The conductor must use the eighth-note beat to control the players, but must not be influenced by the beat, which should be treated here purely as a means of coordinating the players. In fact, attempting to maintain a steady beat throughout the bar is likely to distract the conductor from identifying fully with the dramatic shape of the musical phrases. As a general rule, it is best to hold back the tempo just before a significant harmonic change or dynamic climax.

Within the 6/8 pattern, the beats that control actual musical events should be well-prepared, while the remaining beats should be only slightly indicated. The student should make every effort not to be under the control of a steady pulse, and should focus instead on creating the dramatic shape and inner tension of the musical phrases.

Tristan und Isolde

Prelude

Richard Wagner

Debussy, Prélude à l'après-midi d'un faune

This example also calls for considerable tempo flexibility within the phrase. It is a good exercise in conducting 6/8, 9/8 and 12/8 patterns. Treat the latter two patterns as subdivided 3 and subdivided 4, respectively. Bar 6 can be conducted simply by stopping on the downbeat, without going through the 6/8 pattern. An accelerando is implied beginning at bar 14, followed by a ritardando at bar 20. The student should experiment with beating dotted quarters (in 3) from bar 16 to bar 19, returning to eighths in bar 20.

Prélude à l'après-midi d'un faune

Claude Debussy

Puccini, La Bohème - Mi chiamano Mimi

The first bar should be conducted in 4, with an eighth-note subdivision of the last beat. The following 2/4 should be conducted in eighths. Beginning in bar 15, conduct quarter notes then return to conducting eighths in bar 26. Bar 31 begins a fast 2 beat. Bar 49 returns to the slower 4.

This is an exercise in accompaniment. It requires careful, ongoing attention to the soloist (either from a CD recording or performed live), and the ability to follow, and sometimes anticipate, the nuances of the singer's tempi. Moving quickly through the first three beats of bars 3, 4 and 5 allows you to be ready for whatever the singer does at the ends of these bars. Be sure not to rebound after the first beat of bars 36 and 46, as this will cause the players to anticipate the second beat. Listen carefully to the singer's consonants in the ensuing four chords, and try to make the beats coincide with the vowels. Bars 39 and 40 should be given quickly as single "dead" beat downbeats.

La Bohème
Mi chiamano Mimì

Giacomo Puccini

179

APPENDIX A

Glossary of Terms

accelerando (It.)	gradually increasing speed of beat or tempo
Adagio (It.)	slow tempo, between *Largo* and *Andante*
adagissimo (It.)	extremely slow tempo
a due, a2 (It.)	two on a part, unison (usually found in wind or brass parts)
affettuoso (It.)	affectionately
agitato (It.)	in an agitated or excited manner
al Fine (It.)	to the end (*D. C. al Fine* – from the beginning to the end)
Allegretto (It.)	moderately quick, not as fast as *Allegro*
Allegro (It.)	fast tempo
Allargando (It.)	slowing down
Andante (It.)	somewhat slow and relaxed tempo
arco (It.)	with the bow, used in string music following *pizzicato*
assai (It.)	"very" (*Allegro assai* – very fast)
a tempo (It.)	return to normal tempo, usually after *ritardando* or *fermata*
attacca (It.)	indication at the end of a movement that the next movement should follow without pause
belebt (Gr)	animated, lively
belebend (Gr)	animating
cantabile (It.)	in a singing manner
con, col, coll', colla (It.)	"with" (*col legno* – with the wood of a bow; *con brio* – with vigor)
come prima (It.)	as at first
crescendo, cresc. (It.)	getting louder (abbreviated <)
decrescendo, decresc. (It.)	getting softer (abbreviated >)
da capo, D. C. (It.)	"from the top" (used in repeats)
diminuendo, dim. (It.)	getting softer (cf. *decrescendo*)
divisi, div. (It.)	indicates divided section, usually strings
dolce (It.)	sweetly (softly, when used as a dynamic mark)
espressivo, espress. (It.)	expressively
grave (It.)	slow and solemn
…issimo (It.)	suffix indicating superlative
Langsam (Gr)	slow, slowly
Larghetto (It.)	slow and dignified (less slow than *Largo*)
Largo (It.)	very slow tempo (slower than *Adagio*)
legato (It.)	smooth connection between notes, usually indicated by slurs
leggiero (It.)	lightly
Lent (Fr.)	slow
Lentamente (It.)	slowly
Lento (It.)	slow
lo stesso, l'istesso tempo (It.)	"the same tempo" (used to indicate continuation of same beat value when meter signature changes)
loco (It.)	"in place" (indicates return to notated pitch following *8va* or *8va bassa*)
meno (It.)	"less" (*meno mosso* – less motion, slower)
Moderato (It.)	moderate tempo (*Andante moderato* is less slow than *Andante*)
molto (It.)	"very" (*Molto Moderato* – very moderato tempo)
mosso (It.)	"motion" (*più mosso* – more motion, faster)

moto (It.)	"motion" (*con moto* – with motion, hurrying along)
non tanto (It.)	not a lot (*Andante non tanto quasi Moderato*)
più (It.)	"more" (*Più Allegro* – faster)
pizzicato, pizz. (It.)	plucked, in string writing
poco, un poco (It.)	"little" (*un poco più mosso* – a little faster)
poco a poco (It.)	little by little (often used with *accelerando* or *crescendo*)
ponticello (It.)	bridge of a stringed instrument (*sul ponticello* – play with the bow at the bridge)
Presto (It.)	extremely fast tempo (*Prestissimo* – as fast as possible)
punta d'arco (It.)	at the point of the bow
quasi (It.)	"as if", in the style of; "somewhat"
rallentando, rall. (It.)	getting slower (cf. *ritardando*)
rinforzando, rf, rfz, rinf. (It.)	sudden stress (*sforzando*) or sudden, short *crescendo*
ritardando, rit., ritard. (It.)	getting slower by degrees
ritenuto, riten. (It.)	suddenly at a slower tempo
rubato (It.)	elasticity of tempo
sempre (It.)	"always" (*sempre legato* – maintaining a *legato* style)
senza (It.)	"without" (opposite of *con*)
sforzando (It.)	sharp accent
simile (It.)	indication to continue in the same manner
solo, soli (It.)	single part, single parts
sordino, sordini (It.)	"mute, mutes" (*con sord.* – play with a mute)
sostenuto (It.)	"sustained"
sotto voce (It.)	with subdued sound
spiccato (It.)	bouncing the bow on the strings
staccato (It.)	short, separated notes, contrasted with *legato*
stringendo (It.)	squeezing together (a rapid *accelerando* with a *crescendo*)
subito, sub. (It.)	"suddenly" (*subito piano* – suddenly soft)
sul (It.)	"on" (*sul G* – on the G string; *sul tasto* – on the fingerboard)
Tempo giusto (It.)	strict tempo
tenuto, ten. (It.)	fully sustained note, sometimes given slightly longer duration (often represented by a dash above or below the note)
tremolo (It.)	quick reiteration of the same note, usually strings
Tres Modéré (Fr.)	very restrained or moderate
troppo (It.)	"too much" (*Allegro non troppo* – fast, but not too fast)
tutti (It.)	"all" (after "*solo*", indicates resumption of entire section)
vibrato (It.)	playing in a tremulous manner, primarily to add luster to the tone
Vivace (It.)	very fast tempo
voce, voci (It.)	"voices, voices" (*a due voci* –for two instrumental voices)
zart, (Gr)	"tenderly"

APPENDIX B

Dynamic and Articulation Marks

Term	Symbol	Description
staccato		Detached (dot above or below note)
semi-staccato		Audible separation (horizontal dash above or below note)
staccatissimo		Very short and detached (vertical wedge above or below note)
legato		Slur above or below group of notes (strings play under one bow; woodwinds and brass play under one breath)
piano	p	Soft
pianissimo	pp	Very soft
pianississimo	ppp	Extremely soft
mezzo piano	mp	Medium soft
mezzo forte	mf	Medium loud
forte	f	Loud
fortissimo	ff	Very loud
fortississimo	fff	Extremely loud
crescendo	$<$	Gradually growing louder
decrescendo	$>$	Gradually growing softer
accent	$>$	Emphasis on a particular note
marcato	$\wedge$	Marked emphasis on a particular note (stronger than accent)
sforzando	sfz	Very forced
forzando	fz	Forced
fermata	⌢	hold
metronome marking	(♩=60)	Note value = speed
upbow	V	Upbow mark for stings
downbow	⊓	Downbow mark for strings
Octave higher	8va	Play octave higher than written
Octave lower	8vb	Play octave lower than written
ten., tenuto	*ten.*	Hold note to full value, sometimes even longer

APPENDIX C

Transposition

Transposition is necessary so instruments can be built in different keys without requiring performers to learn different fingerings for each key. For example, the English Horn is built in the key of F, but has the same fingerings as the Oboe, which is built in the key of C. This means that the fingering that produces concert C on the Oboe will produce concert F on the English Horn. Writing the English Horn part one fifth higher than the intended pitch allows the English Horn player to use the same fingerings as the Oboe. The English Horn's written C, therefore, sounds as a concert F.

Transposing instruments are usually identified as being "in" a particular key (such as Clarinet *in* B flat). This always means that the instrument's written C will sound as the concert pitch of the key of the instrument (as in a B-flat Clarinet's C will sound as a concert B flat).

See the table below for transposing Instruments.

Instrument	Written	Sounds
Piccolo in C sounds an octave higher than written		
Alto Flute in G sounds a perfect fourth lower than written		
English Horn in F sounds a perfect fifth lower than written		
Clarinet in E flat sounds a minor third higher than written		
Clarinet in D sounds a major second higher than written		
Clarinet in B flat sounds a major second lower than written		
Clarinet in A sounds a minor third lower than written		
Alto Clarinet in E flat (sounds a major sixth lower than written		
Basset Horn in F alto clarinet in F, sounds a perfect fifth lower than written		
Bass Clarinet in B flat when in treble clef, sounds a major ninth lower than written; when in bass clef, sounds a major second lower than written		
Bass Clarinet in A when in treble clef, sounds a minor tenth lower than written; when in bass clef, sounds a minor third lower than written)		
Contra-Alto Clarinet in E flat sounds an octave and a major sixth lower than written		
Contrabass Clarinet in B flat sounds two octaves and a major second lower than written		
Contrabassoon sounds an octave lower than written		

Horn in F modern notation: treble or bass clef – sounds a perfect fifth lower than written; earlier notation: sounds a perfect fifth lower then written in treble clef	Horn in F	Horn in F
Piccolo Trumpet in B flat sounds a minor seventh higher than written	Piccolo Trumpet	Piccolo Trumpet
Trumpet in D sounds a major second higher than written	Trumpet in D	Trumpet in D
Trumpet in B flat sounds a major second lower than written	Trumpet in B♭	Trumpet in B♭
Trumpet in F found in early 20th century scores; sounds a perfect fourth higher than written	Trumpet in F	Trumpet in F
Baritone Horn, Euphonium when in treble clef, sounds a minor ninth lower than written; when in bass clef, sounds as written	Euphonium	Euphonium
String Bass sounds an octave lower than written	Double Basses	Double Basses
Celeste, Glockenspiel, Xylophone sounds one or more octaves higher than written	Glockenspiel	Glockenspiel
Choral Tenors Treble clef, but sounds an octave lower than written. Sometimes written in tenor clef at actual pitch	Tenor Solo	Tenor Solo

Clefs

Treble Clef	G = second line up	
Alto Clef	C = middle line	
Tenor Clef	C = fourth line up	
Bass Clef	F = fourth line up	

Instruments and Clefs

- Piccolo, Flute, Oboe, English Horn, Clarinet, Saxophone, Trumpet and Violin always use treble clef.

- Bass Clarinet, Euphonium, and Baritone Horn can be written in either bass or treble clef. Treble clefs transpose differently than bass clefs (see Appendix C).

- Violas normally are written in the alto clef, although they may also use the treble clef. Earlier scores often use the alto clef for the first trombone as well.

- Bassoon, Contrabassoon, Trombone, Cello, and String Bass normally are written in bass clef. Occasionally, they may be written in tenor clef or even treble clef. In older scores (e.g., Tchaikovsky), cellos are sometimes written in treble clef, but are intended to sound an octave below written pitch. In modern scores, cellos written in treble clef are intended to sound as written. String Basses and Contrabassoons written in tenor or treble clefs sound an octave lower than written.

- Choral music written during the Baroque and Classical periods are occasionally still published using mezzo and baritone clefs. Mezzo clefs (used for second sopranos) have the middle C as the bottom line; baritone clefs have middle C as the top line.

Use the table below for quick reference

Instruments	Clef
Piccolo Flute Oboe English Horn Clarinet Saxophone Trumpet Violin	𝄞
Bass Clarinet Baritone Horn Euphonium	𝄢 or 𝄞
Viola	𝄡 sometimes 𝄞
Trombone	𝄢 sometimes 𝄡 𝄡 𝄞
Bassoon Contrabassoon Cello String Bass	𝄢 occasionally 𝄡 𝄞